PARTING SORROWS

Edited by

CHRIS WALTON

First published in Great Britain in 1998 by
TRIUMPH HOUSE
1-2 Wainman Road, Woodston,
Peterborough, PE2 7BU
Telephone (01733) 230749

All Rights Reserved

Copyright Contributors 1998

HB ISBN 1 86161 254 0
SB ISBN 1 86161 259 1

FOREWORD

Poetry is a creative art form and a great medium for communication - now becoming more widely recognised and received.
Poets from all over the world have come together in this special anthology of creative work to express their emotions, faith and hopes they have for the future.

Each poem is connected in some way and the styles used and themes conveyed complement each other wonderfully.

Together a unique collection of Christian poetry has been created that offers the reader a great wealth of inspiration and an insight into the Christian faith.

Editor
Chris Walton

CONTENTS

Absolution	Yasmeen Ahmed	1
Surgery	Ian Fowler	2
Annihilation	Maureen Atkin	4
Heaven Or Hell	Nikki Mortimer	5
Water In England	Janice Tucker	6
The Twilight	Jennifer Abdulazeez	7
UFOs	Mabel Helen Underwood	8
Inner Fire	Ann Voaden	9
One Bowl of Grain?	Rose M Cooper	10
The Universal Lottery	Sheila Margaret Parker	11
A New Earth	Alec Williams	12
Rainfall In Africa	Una Rutledge	14
Close To The Edge	Patrick B Osada	15
The Lost Place	Maggi L T MacLeod	16
He Hangeth The World Upon Nothing Job 26.7	Jane Freeman	17
Epitaph To Emily	David Barrow	18
Money - And All That Jazz	Paul Gold	19
Destruction Of A Race - A Poem In Five Parts	C Smith	20
Glad - The Wool Gatherer	Georgina Francis McKellar	22
Night Sky	D C Bollen	23
Windows	Peter Stock	24
New Land	Julia Garvey	25
A Heavenly Dream	Beatrice Wilson	26
Judgement Day	Elaine Hawkins	28
The Heartbreak Of War	Gordon Rainey	29
Would You Walk In My Shoes?	Sally Malone	30
Art	Roy Storey	31
Bridge Of The Gods	Freda Baxter	32
Prayer From The Dying	Jan Lingard	33
Filth Of Time	Kevin Michael Jones	34
Images	E Jones	35
Beyond Thought . . .	Stephen Gyles	36
A Girl Sits Under The Baobab Tree	Jan Ingram McCaffery	37

The Mill	S Chandler	38
Imagine	Melita Colton	39
Until You Come Again	John Christopher	40
Whose Funeral?	Simon Warren	41
The Edge Of Silence	S Chesterman	42
Arlecs Anguish	Carole Beodricks Worth Reynolds	43
Footprints	Margaret Black	44
Southern Alberta In The Fall	David Tallach	45
Cheltenham	P Edwards	46
Land Without Childhood	J Facchini	47
The Ocean Road	Gwendoline Douglas	48
The Monsoons	Richard J Bradshaw	49
Fish Eye	Nick Colton	50
Beyond The Horizon	Elsie Norman	51
Whisky 2	Elaine McCulloch Smith	52
Regency Lady	Caron Hunt	53
Decree Nisi	David Watson	54
Street Child	Linda J Bodicoat	55
The Aboriginee	Mary Rutley	56
The Lamb Of Knock	Jean Turner	57
The Old White Lion Hotel (Haworth)	Christopher Rothery	58
Beyond The Horizon	Don Mayle	59
A Spider Spins His Web	H A M	60
Beyond Our Horizon?	Mary Ryan	61
The Whirling Wheels	Ian Barton	62
Beyond The Horizon	Keely Pepper	63
Sizewell B	Tina Brewer	64
The Bittern's Way	Dennis Marshall	66
Yellow Belly Custard	Kenneth Butler	67
Northern Sung	Guy Brown	68
To Boldly Go	Michael Darwood	69
Space And Beyond	Kofi Oduro-A	70
Two Worlds - Hawaii And England	Barbara Hickman	71
The Bell Of The Datura	Sandra Lewis	72
The Great Staircase	Evelyn Balmain	73

Millennium Madness	R Castleton	74
Their Story . . . Lives	Jamuna Charles	75
AD 79	Maurice Bowler	76
Millennium Dome - Thoughts Of An Old, Homeless Person	Anne Leahy	77
Worship	Sister Magdalen	78
The Abyss Of Loneliness	Pauline Uprichard	79
Beyond The Horizon	Ann Copland	80
Mount Sarno	Rita Fisher	81
Tudor Court	Christopher Johnson	82
Scene In Sudan	Pauline Pullan	83
A Man Sat By The Well	Pauline Wilkins	84
Noah's Neighbour	Dan Pugh	85
Naumi	P J Littlefield	86
Time Evolves	Doris Hoole	88
Magic Carpet	Margaret Gardner	89
Heartache	Dorothy Woodward	90
Floating (Helicon)	Tilla B Smith	91
The Force	Iolo Lewis	92
Needs Must	Anne Trapp	93
Columbus	A K S Shaw	94
From Cradle To Grave	Edward Roberts	96
The Land Of The Scorching Sun	Ruth Daviat	97
Childhood Reflections	Barbara Crook	98
Millennium	Maurice Wilkinson	99
Drifting	Nicole Purkiss	100
The Berlin Wall	Gordon Haines	101
Hunger Of The African Plain	Lindsey Maggs	102
Beyond The Horizon	Rebecca Lawrence	103
What Is Presence?	Melynie Smith	104
After The Earthquake	Barbara King	105
Rwanda	Ray Moore	106
Emotional Freedom	Alan Jones	107
Peace	Margaret White	108
ET's Son	Colin Allsop	109
Producing Manure	Paul Corrigan	110
Children Of Africa	Jane Otieno	111
Glory	Jade Draven	112

Everest	Dora Stables	113
Sarigerme, Turkey	A T Williams	114
Beyond Consciousness	Raymond Fenech	115
Beyond The Horizon	Jean P McGovern	116
The Lost Planet	J Russell	117

ABSOLUTION

Is it my fault?
In love and affection
The world is deficient
And a world without rules
With abuse of every kind
War, hunger, rape, genocide
Young nor old are safe.

Eclipse love and affection
With no expression, nothing to express.

Humans and animals all gifted with love
Then why this? Or is it truly my fault?

Incessant are love and affection
But I'm left barren covet suppression.

If benevolent world in lieu of evil
Could time heal or goodness defeat evil?

Too trivial a retrieval
I'm betrayed beyond
Like hot lava engulfed
No absolution for me.

Yasmeen Ahmed

Surgery

As I am lying on the table
I start to look around
The place seems so empty
I listen but I can't hear a single sound.

It is an eerie feeling
Scarier than you can imagine
As they ask you your name once more
And gently wheel you in.

Then they produce the needle
Which will send you to sleep
You feel absolutely nothing
As you gently start to weep.

They ask you to count from one hundred
You never reach ninety eight
As you gently drift away
With someone else deciding your fate.

Some time later you wake to find
People standing over you
All saying how wonderful it is
That you pulled through.

The physical scars may
Heal all fine and well
But what about the emotional ones
Who can really tell?

For it is a real trauma
Operation after operation
No one is asking for favours
But our feelings deserve some consideration.

I know that what I am saying
To some people may cause offence
But unless you have suffered
You don't know what we experience.

People think that they know
But I don't see how they can
For unless you have ever been there
How can you really ever understand?

Ian Fowler

ANNIHILATION

I struggle to digest the news:
'One day remains ere man's demise.'
I comprehend, yet still refuse
to accept that - beyond these skies -
an earthbound meteorite flies
en route for direct impact. *Mere
comic caper!* Plots and foul lies
of enemies strike greater fear.

But words are neither jest nor ruse.
Accepting truth, I agonise,
then devise plans for rendezvous
with family, whose heartfelt sighs,
intense embrace and fraught goodbyes
cause need to staunch a welling tear.
Though death impends, would hostile eyes
of enemies strike greater fear?

Dread of the day that I might lose
my partner - for love's bond still ties
our hearts - recedes. Bereft I'd *choose*
to die. Distress preoccupies.
Annihilation's onslaught vies
with anguished thoughts of those most dear.
Life's end draws nigh . . . did vengeful cries
of enemies strike greater fear?

Now firmament turmoil implies
impact proximity, it's clear
that *acts of God* - not weapon size
of enemies - strike greater fear.

Maureen Atkin

HEAVEN OR HELL

It's five hundred years since I walked on this earth
I was frozen in time fifteen years from my birth,
So many questions many answers to find
In a world so alien to my human mind,

Who put me here, and how when and why,
I had no importance, why did I not die?
Am I just an experiment: like a rat in a cage?
Are you reading my thoughts: do you feel my rage?

Tell me, am I in heaven or am I in hell?
Am I really here, or am I under some spell?
I just want to see you; confirm that you're real,
My fear is controlling the way that I feel.

There's a presence here but I see no face,
Are you friend or foe that abides in this place?
I open my eyes, is that a mirror I see?
I'm afraid of the eyes staring back at me.

I hear cold laughter, it's all around
It reminds me of a familiar sound,
And just when I think I may be set free
I look up and discover the voice is *me!*

Nikki Mortimer

WATER IN ENGLAND...
(Dedicated to Alexander Evan)

We are so lucky in England,
and, although we have to pay,
we have fresh water
available every day.

A lot of countries don't have this,
yet we take it for granted.
It is so useful though,
it is something we need.

We do not have to pump
our water by hand.
We have it by tap,
to cope with our demands.

We don't have to travel for it,
it comes to our homes.
Some people have to travel miles,
but when there's a water ban we moan.

So next time you have the tap on,
have a little think about
the countries who have little water
through having so many droughts.

Janice Tucker

THE TWILIGHT

Standing here
By the seashore
The golden beach
Spreading so afar
The shimmering waters
Glistening so alight
In an instant
Fascinating and beckoning
Beyond the floating waters
Arise the *twilight*
Astring with colour
Alike the rainbow
Aglow with a rosy hue
Like the dust of dreams
Soon it will be cloaky dark
for a tomorrow
With another beauty of nature
Called - *the twilight.*

Jennifer Abdulazeez

UFOs

When tapering rays of sunlight reach above
        The dimmed horizon, streaking up the sky,
        I sometimes wait until their fingers die
Or disappear, as in a darkened glove,
        And watch the distant stars intensify.

I wonder how they all began, and when -
        Or if - the universe will ever end;
        And are there really planets there, which send
What we call UFOs here, time and again,
        And if so, what *on earth* do they intend?

They must be friendly for, with such great skill
        And knowledge, far beyond man's puny art -
        Which in space quest has barely made a start -
They could impose on Earth their conquering will,
        Yet only seem to appear and then depart.

If they are wondering what we think of them,
        Then what *on other planets* do they plan?
        How does their intellect pass that of man?
Can it from some weird early creature's stem,
        As Hawking's goes beyond Earth's first caveman?

And so we trust they really wish us well,
        Are only showing interest in our state,
        And trying to understand how man can hate
His brother man. Perhaps they strive to tell
        Us more of God, who did all worlds create.

Mabel Helen Underwood

INNER FIRE

Deep within a tumult boils,
tormented earth on heat,
trapped below in fathoms far beyond
old Father Neptune's seat.
Encrusted earth of plates and seams
controlling coastal shape,
hidden power of nature's inner wrath
preparing surface rape.
Deep within a tumult boils,
seething mass of fire
trapped below in depths past mortal reach
and never does it tire;
Nature's infernal core of life,
embodied gaseous fumes
forming, shaping, spewing forth
when all else it exhumes.
We are at nature's mercy,
we are at nature's call,
succumbing all our mortal frame
for we cannot conquer all.
Nature formed us from the dust
and to the dust return
our bodies, back to earthen core
when we have had our turn;
Only our souls defy the fray,
our 'self' we can control
and needs must quench human baser fires,
to purify the whole.

Ann Voaden

ONE BOWL OF GRAIN?

One bowl of grain is all we can spare -
For the shadows of humanity, living out there?
Too weary to cry, walking for miles in vain
Too weary to cry, bowed with sorrow and pain.

One bowl of grain is all we can allow -
The eyes - sunken wells beneath the brow -
Wide, deep brown eyes staring - hoping for more
But what can one do with an empty store?

Haunted by the sights we see - bodies drawn taut by famine and fear
We cry 'Lord send precious healing water here.'
For he only has *our* hands to ease the pain
In a world which has gone completely insane.

Show me what I ought to do, to help my brothers in distress
Give them just a little more - I can manage with so much less
Let people see part of the Christ in me, living as You would have me be
Then might the world far happier be with everyone looking unto Thee!
Sharing with others, then can we dare to say
'Give *us* our daily bread each day.'

Rose M Cooper

THE UNIVERSAL LOTTERY

Clean fresh underwear every day
Baths and showers to wash my cares away
A car to drive and freedom to roam
Living well fed in a modern home
While running fresh water taps at the sink
My thoughts travel and I start to think
Of other women so far away
In a different country and culture to me
The African standing with child all bare
Hungry, nay starving, a vacant stare
Nothing to stimulate, no future, no mirth
Daily fight for survival on this planet Earth
And though we ease our consciences
With gifts to charity
It's too little too late
For the depths of depravity
Through the TV screen you sit and stare
Shrivelled breasts to suckle your child
Flies crawling on your face and hair
Sadly, I have to come to terms
That this is what is meant to be
While travelling the journey of our lives
This passage of time in the universal lottery.

Sheila Margaret Parker

A New Earth

A new horizon I have seen
where all of man is squeaky clean,
the sky is no more shades of blue
a rainbow starts each day anew.
War is just a word in books
and no one gives out racial looks,
the children play in twos and threes
but still a plaster fits grazed knees.
being at work is just so simple
The boss he smiles and shows his dimple,
no pressures, only easy ways
an hour's work brings six pay days.
The sun gives rays from morn till night,
at noon it throws a bright pink light.
It also shines at midnight too,
the greenest parks turn deepest blue.
The food is great and plentiful,
all nations live, by spiritual,
in favour of the God most high,
who took old Earth up to His sky.
He brought about this paradise
and gave it to His son the Christ,
by His hand we live and learn
He governs and shares our concerns.
Now we have a ruling king,
His righteousness we daily sing
if together all can be,
together we'll sail the open sea,
If to hold each other dear,
of course my love we'll have no fear.
The tidings of a better path
more time to share, grin and laugh.

A peaceful place of astounding merriment,
on animals, there'd be no lab experiments
which need performing by doctor's hands,
and by so caring save many a grand.
If this place was here with me,
there'd be no need to future see.

Alec Williams

Rainfall In Africa

Continuous pounding on corrugated roofs,
Sun-baked earth sliced into slushy rivulets,
Out of red soil, termites oozing in procession,
Find themselves easy prey for starving cats and dogs.
Heavy hard-backed beetles wriggling upside down,
Struggling to regain their slippery footholds.
And in little African huts, happy people
Silencing the pleading staccato beat of drums,
The harvest now ensured by heaven's answer.

Una Rutledge

CLOSE TO THE EDGE

Before the shrieking flashed the buzzing hummed
And in the darkness grew the sound of birds.
Into my sightless space a fluttering crashed -
Silence exploding: the singing night heard.

Around is the blueness of air and water,
Below and above the sea melts sky:
Liquids of air, fused on the mountain top,
Sparkle and gleam on the valley floor.
From each blue valley ripples are floating
Flooding the plains to cascade down
Upon mountains below, where air meets water;
Close to the edge, in passing dreams I go.

Patrick B Osada

THE LOST PLACE

There is a lost place within
I stand outside and weep.
The trivia of living
surrounds and confounds
inducing world weariness.

I stand at the edge of the stars
and see complete confusion.
A few calm corners
shine bluely
and I wish to bind them
all together into
a bright band of friendship.

I cannot bear to
hear the myriad voices and opinions
raised to so-called good deeds and gladness.

I feel the wrath of God within
and would rant and rave at them
but they would never know
that they should listen
and follow
to the lost place within.

The world seems to me to be a pinpoint,
the small dot upon the page

and I am soaring in a
fearful awareness.

Maggi L T MacLeod

HE HANGETH THE WORLD UPON NOTHING JOB 26.7

I believe I thought when flesh wore thin
And muscle stringy
The clutch of time's fell hand would hook
Each to all since each refused
To accord oblivion to our sort
Beyond the grave. And communication
Through goods acquired as things of worth
Would outlast the family fate.

As the years incise my skin
With unplanned wrinkles,
Scoring deep on sullied looks
The wear and tear of overuse,
Delving the parallels of thought
Above a repeated conversation,
I reappraise the patch of earth
That firmed the family face.

Old, detached from kith and kin;
Differently single;
Undeterred by the bell, the book
And candle of their hurt abuse,
I turn with joy to the lovely noughts
Of nothing which holds up creation
Where seamless time and space give birth
To ignorance of place.

Jane Freeman

Epitaph To Emily

Where her voice is still remembered,
in the church, in which she worshipped.
Where she stood apart from the choir.
She does not sing hymns any more.

Gazing sun looks in through windows,
lighting up rows of empty pews,
where echoes inside, confessed sins
forgiven by God, long since past.

Quietly, she lies in the grave.
She has found a life eternal
and can sing her hymns to Heaven,
while angels listen in the wind.

David Barrow

MONEY - AND ALL THAT JAZZ

They say that I am too easy-going with money
They remark - because I always pick up the tabs -
That my public tipping is far too generous
To waiters, porters and drivers of taxi-cabs.

On the question of being too free with money
My answer is 'Why not? All my life I've had lots and lots
It's my way of helping those a little *short of the ready*
Those unfortunates they call the *have-nots*.

In my club, I am shunned by some of the local wealthy
They resent my friendship with people of lesser means,
Personally I don't give a monkey's - this is me
Maybe it's hereditary, maybe it's something in my genes.

An old school friend wrote to me with problems
He was deeply in debt, right up to his neck,
Although our Oxford days were now just a memory
What the heck! I sent him a generous cheque.

I gave a donation to my ailing third division football club
They offered me the chairmanship - plus a seat on the board,
However I had only sent a mere half-a-million.
Why, to sit on that board, I would feel a bit of a fraud.

Last month, my numbers came up correctly on the National Lottery
Flush with excitement? I certainly was not.
They say that some winners really go bananas
Stupid people, so they won a few million - so what?

They say that you can't take it with you
How true! What use is money up there?
And, 'tis rumoured, that heavenly inmates play Rummy for marbles
And for starters, 'He' checks that everyone gets the same share.

Paul Gold

DESTRUCTION OF A RACE - A POEM IN FIVE PARTS

Human Reasoning (I)

The stars they stare from the darkened sky,
Upon this world which peace does lie,
And comes the rising of the sun of past,
And so the shadow of death is cast.
The world awakes with the pending dawn
To bring to eyes destruction and more,
For within the limits of called humanity,
We fought for our lives to be free,
And losing our sanity in our haste,
Brought about the destruction of our race.

Aftermath (II)

Around me lies a desolate, barren land,
With fire and flame close at hand,
People screaming, crying in pain,
Yet any help is totally in vain,
For death is soon to come and call,
For the very last of us all.

Awaiting Death (III)

Choking on the red hot heat,
It's now deliverance we desperately seek,
Burning, blindness is still to come,
Though death is quick for the lucky some.
There is no food upon which to feed,
Even if we should find the need.
But over most death does loom
And will claim its victims fairly soon.

Freedom From Greed (IV)

I hope I'm one of the lucky few,
That death is kind and takes me too,
For dying and pain are all I can see,
And my only wish is to be free,
Of this searching pain upon my skin
Caused by a people's greatest sin,
A need for power, a deadly greed,
For which we no longer have a need.

Remorseful Alone (V)

There'll be no one alive the next morn,
Just a land empty and torn,
Only the scars of death shall remain,
Not the guilt, shame or blame.

C Smith

GLAD - THE WOOL GATHERER

Vest for the orphan, shawl for the old
Each stitch a prayer for those in the cold
Time worn hands painful and stiff
Plying their craft while she wonders if
The dispossessed appreciate a kind heart
Bringing succour against all that man can impart

On painful feet she leaves her chair
She has no time to stop and stare
Another loop, another round
'Ah yes' the exact colour found.
The fingers speed on more hours sitting,
Teasing and winding, crocheting and knitting

Taken - in reels or ends of hanks
With time only for a cursory thanks
Time is wasting so much to do
Winter is nigh another vest or two
Bits of balls and odds and ends
Tying together a myriad of friends

No time for public recognition
Only the collector's admiration
A bundle gone another to start
Her stool balancing the pain of the caring heart
She does not want to die, not yet,
With so many bundles to get.

Georgina Francis McKellar

NIGHT SKY

Encrystalled sky;
I look beyond the trails of travellers
Through dark silence, lit only by cold stars
To where all dreams are reality.

Far from the all-coloured day
Stretches, along a vectored infinity
That which challenges faith.

I am content yet troubled . . .
 . . . by the magnitude of my ignorance.

Rain washes my face but not my mind;
And all sunsets are but beauty endowed
To soothe a restless reasoning.

Caverns open in the dark distance,
And when I gaze into the eyes of the night sky
Nothingness stares back at me
Through angry tears of confusion.

D C Bollen

WINDOWS

Oft have I fled these narrow confines,
Dark with pain, and fettered thoughts,
Through windows beckoning out to freedom
Of wide, wild, windy sea and sky
To far distant realms of fantasy.

I climbed the shimmering, towering cloud caps
To golden castles, wreathed in light,
Where magical, ethereal creatures
Writhed and wrestled
In ceaseless strife.

I peered in purple coated caverns
And watched the lightning play with fire.
I fell, like Lucifer, from heaven,
And skimmed the waves
With showering trails of stars.

I followed speeding winds o'er surging oceans,
And heard the mountains clap uplifted hands,
In singing deserts, mighty voices
Struck the living rocks asunder
And made them flow in restless seas of sand.

I danced with solemn, whirling dervishes
Through cities bright with jewelled fires,
Whose skirts drew sparks uprising
From pavements formed of fallen stars
Caught in a web of fiery flight.

And there I yielded to the turmoil
Of this binding, prisoned pain,
And found an unexpected ease unleashing
A calm tranquility of heart and mind,
A soft and peaceful bed on which to lie.

Peter Stock

NEW LAND

Land of plenty
Land of joy
Safe place for girl or boy
Is it only in hopes and dreams
I see this land so rich and green
wondrous land
with mountains and plains
with crops of wheat, rye and
other grains
A land that cares for old and
young
That listens to others with different
tongues
A land where weapons have no need
A land whose people show no greed
This land I feel comes from the heart
Let's all join together to be a part!

Julia Garvey

A Heavenly Dream

I wandered through the fields of buttercups
amongst the cows and horses in the field.
The air was pure; the sun was shining;
with the fragrant smell of spring which grass
                              and flowers do yield.

The trees were smiling as they waved their branches;
the rabbits and the hares bobbed in the grass.
My father's morgan there, parked in a lay-by,
- What a happy scene in which an hour to pass.

The birds were singing merrily their birdsong;
and now May and I were climbing stile and gate;
My mother had unpacked our picnic basket;
and we were surveying this - as we sat and ate.

Doddy and Bill came walking from the hill
                                  up yonder;
And Fred and Kath were there - hand in hand;
Lost friends and family now all met to gather -
And - in a moment - we were on the sand!

The sea was calm; and we were playing
on the beach - Was this then all yesteryear?
Had this been a dream of my own making?
It seemed like heaven - Was I really there?

Was this a mirage that I had invented,
a childhood memory of days gone by;
The love, the joy in which we were all moulded -
Would I find them again above the sky?

Skip and Bob came racing up to greet me;
Bubbles and Squeak (the budgies) they were there!
Surely this was a foretaste of my heaven,
And I'd find it all again, to lose it ne'er.

Beatrice Wilson

JUDGEMENT DAY

Black river of poison, winds snakelike,
Working its way from inland seeking,
Destination, thick mass of death,
Once abundant life filled sea,
Through land barren, buildings crumble,
What's left, decayed remnants of past humanity,
Across bleak sunless horizon,
Thick grey sky rains white dust,
Mockingly it chokes unyielding land,
Fear is past, no boundaries,
It is judgement day, every day since,
No-one lives above, can't breathe,
The dead are dust, blanketing the ground,
So cold, no atmosphere or humidity,
Hovers this planet,
Carelessly landscaped by man,
This mass execution of existence,
No-one is left to view the horror.

Elaine Hawkins

THE HEARTBREAK OF WAR

A mother gets a telegram, her only son is dead
To hear the postman's footsteps, had filled her heart
With dread, and husband's too complete the story, a
Medal for a life, in the fruitless search for glory -
All that's left, a weeping wife.

Yet it seems it's just accepted, been the same for many
Years, so it's time it was rejected, put an end to all
The tears. If people everywhere refused to fight, they'd
Give the press new words to write, no more words
Like death - decease but better words like joy and peace.

Politicians can't achieve this, though it's true they've often
Tried, but with all their worthless treaties it still
Meant that good men died. If they'd only read their bibles
They'd see the righteous knew, that God can see the future,
So His prophecies come true! The prince of peace has promised
He won't lead us astray. Yes, He has been commissioned by God
To show the way.

The time is coming shortly, He's opened up the door
To fulfil Isaiah's prophecy, that we'll learn war
No more. Then the wolf will dwell with the lamb
The lion eat straw like the bull. As all the earth
Rejoices - in God's peaceful kingdom rule!

Gordon Rainey

WOULD YOU WALK IN MY SHOES?

As you wander the streets of Calcutta
See me sitting, feet in the gutter,
Begging for alms with outstretched palms
Shunned for my limp and my stutter.

Just a raggedy beggar boy
Whose life has no joy,
Do you see the flies that buzz round my eyes
Or this stick that I use as a toy?

I see you pass me everyday
You don't meet my eyes, you just hurry away,
You'd rather not see somebody like me,
A penniless scavenging stray.

But I will survive
And I will contrive,
To cope in the absence of hope,
And despite you I will stay alive.

Sally Malone

ART

The art of politics
is to speak many words.
To people that bleat
or stand around in hordes.
We never use 'I'
We always use 'We'.
It is all for the good
of our country.
We *never* drink,
we *never* smoke,
to have *affair*,
we just don't.
We're whiter than white
so should it be.
For we are the *best*
politically.

Roy Storey

BRIDGE OF THE GODS
(American Indian Legend)

Just for a moment take my hand
and wander through this pleasant land,
the scene of tallest redwoods and waterfalls.
This is the most magical place of all
where, in your imagination, you may see
Sasquatch -Bigfoot - or, lurking behind a tree
Yakima Indian, arrows in his quiver
along the banks of the mighty Columbia River.

The mountains, like St Helens' volcanic hell
have many mysteries to tell
of long before the dollar or the dime,
legends of Indian ancestors' time
and Dreamweaver, conjuring up the spirits
to heal the sick, or cast a spell.

Two of them -Mt Adams and Mt Hood,
their spirits being misunderstood
because, Indian brothers they had been
but turned into mountains in a fiery scene
by angry Gods, who watched them from above,
as they battled for Sleeping Beauty Mountain's love.
From a 'natural' stone bridge, the tumbled rocks
formed the narrowed Cascade Locks.

The gods had built this bridge of stone
between Washington and Oregon
but today, further along in history,
a steel bridge is there for all to see.
So where the north-west traveller plods
strange tales surround the Bridge of the Gods
which an eerie mist always enshrouds
and whispers are heard from above the clouds.

Freda Baxter

Prayer From The Dying

Take me, please, down to the water
And let me lay
Where once I'd play.
Hold me gently, whisper to me
Once again
To ease my pain.
Talk to me of happy moments
When first we met;
Or better yet
Sing to me of parting sorrow.
Soothe my fears
Yet shed no tears.
My soul is caught, a netted creature,
In this useless shell.
My living hell.
My time grows short as sickness claims me,
So offer me
Some dignity.
As the wind-whipped waves are softly lapping
On our sea-kissed shore,
Let me breathe no more.
No fear have I of endless darkness,
I befriend it.
Please, help me end it.

Jan Lingard

FILTH OF TIME

The kitchen sink was full
of greasy pots
waiting to be washed,
but no fairy came
the dining table had ring marks
upon its surface
made by the teacups
but Mr Sheen was never seen.
The cooker was covered in
a greasy grime,
which gathered over
a period of time.
The fridge had seen better days
but now it looked a shadow
of its former self
with rust spots all over.
The once sparkling window pane
was covered in industrial grey,
cobwebs hung from the ceiling
slowly swaying from side to side
not wishing to hide.
The carpet yearned for the hoover
to ride over its dusty plains
but the hoover too was a
non-mover.
The automatic washer door was
open wide,
with washing still inside,
an ambience of melancholy
was now the dweller,
for long has passed the glory days
when housework was its slave.

Kevin Michael Jones

IMAGES

The creativity of visions
Technology at play
Virtual reality
A world of fantasy
Relax with visor over eyes
Focus of the scene
Weightless, transformation rise
Projected on the screen
This doorway to another world
Ready, activate
Panoramic landscapes
Transmit, communicate
Transparent colours variate, transfiguration flick
Before my eyes, strange designs
Silently, so quick
Escapism, euphoria, sensations that excite
This illusionary journey, images in flight
Physical perception perforates the mind
Dimension in another world
Connected and entwined
Return back to reality from cybernetic themes
Or virtual technology and futuristic dreams.

E Jones

BEYOND THOUGHT...

My brain is in overdrive
as I hunt the elusive particles
and battle the unruly numbers
frantically trying to form
equations to evolve and discover
a Grand Unified Theory.

How little we really know
of ourselves, the earth, the sun,
the planets, the galaxies
and the evolving expanding universe.
So let our ignorance
speed us upon our cosmic quest.

We must discover our future
by gaining wisdom and knowledge
to uncover the secrets of the universe
which are hidden from us
in the deep dark surging
chaotic seas of space...

Then we will comprehend
our place in the cosmic scheme
and follow the pathway of the stars
until we reach a singularity
beyond space time... beyond matter
beyond words, beyond thoughts...

For the moment I have failed
to find the symbols
that I need to formulate
a theory of all and everything
but what remains a cosmic dream
will one day be reality...

Stephen Gyles

A GIRL SITS UNDER THE BAOBAB TREE

I know a village in Africa
Where the huts are round and the ground is bare,
A girl sits under the baobab tree
Guarding her goats and sheep.

This isn't Happy Valley.

When the rains don't come
In the burning sun
Crops shrivel up, animals get thin,
People can starve and die.

Wayna Kithone writes in thick pencil
And sends her letters on airmail paper
'My school has a tank but there's not enough water,
This year the cattle are sick.'

In Kasasi her parents learn husbandry,
Cross-breeding goats with different animals,
Controlling pests carried by ticks
To stop the spread of disease.

So we send her money to buy her shoes,
For farming tools and education,
But is this enough for the girl who sits
In beaded braids
Under the baobab tree.

This isn't Happy Valley.

When the rains don't come
In the burning sun
Crops shrivel up, animals get thin,
People can starve and die.

Jan Ingram McCaffery

THE MILL

Lying so still, no longer used
>The mill in the village stands
No sound of the wheels grinding
>The grain from of farmers' lands

The sails used to turn
>Casting their shadows
On my bedroom wall
>Making pictures
To entertain me
>Long ago, when I was small

If I sit still, and close my eyes
>I can see it, working once more
Hear the horses, delivering grain
>And the creek of the old mill door

Hear the sound of the sails turning
>Grinding the grain into flour
Living life at a nice even pace
>No rush to be home on the hour.

S Chandler

IMAGINE

Imagine an image, an image
So small, an image so tall,
Imagine.

Imagine an image, an image
So wide, an image with pride,
Imagine.

Melita Colton

Until You Come Again

If man could learn to cast aside
his need for greater power,
and turned instead to Jesus Christ
the world could change this hour.

If man could just be satisfied
and disregarded greed,
he'd surely find his peace in One
who answers every need.

If man stopped being envious
and learned to be content,
then he would know far greater joy
and envy would be spent.

Lord, power and greed and envy are
the recipes for war,
and if man changed his attitude
there would be peace once more.

Views must be altered. Man must see
he has to compromise,
but if he'd come in faith to You
how great would be his prize!

So many folk with silent voice
are victims, cast to fate,
and man impatiently strides on
for progress cannot wait!

We pray dear Lord, that very soon
Your Sovereign power will reign,
and man will learn to live in love
until You come again.

John Christopher

WHOSE FUNERAL?

Waiting by night
Waiting until the life of the day is over
Waiting for the time
When the General's meal will be over
When for the rest of the night
The General will sleep with his wife
Near his children
Who are so dear to him
However
Not tonight General
This is the General's routine
As the lights go out in the Cairo Hilton
There's a weak link
Between Special Branch
Liaising with the Military Police
For one widow this Wednesday
Ali or was it Mohamed
Kid the gun was passed to me
In the casbah
In the light which was failing
With it a new box of ammunition
Wait?
I've been waiting all my life
Just for the General
There's a penumbra
Around the General's head
The light of the entrance
A perfect target
For an Ingram Mac 10
To find.

Simon Warren

THE EDGE OF SILENCE

Entering the edge of silence
My senses start to fade
All I hear is nothing
And my eyes see only grey

Shadows flicker in the distance
Can't hear a word they say
Have I been alone too long
Or forgotten what to say

This night has been a long one
By morning I'll be better
Being idle doesn't mean
I can't enjoy my leisure

If I don't speak to anyone
Then they won't speak to me
All I'll have is silence
And tranquillity

Should somebody say move
I'll ask the reason why
For if I am happy here
Then here I shall die

When I can't see anybody
Then nobody exists
Silence is my companion
Here in my emptiness.

S Chesterman

ARLECS ANGUISH

After fifteen long years, of a pretty pointless, hostile war,
Two years' existence spent without a drop of much needed rain,
Today Southern Sudan's imminent bleak future is faced,
With widespread famine, poverty, disease for many unrelenting pain,
Every day the long trail of Sudanese women, carrying clay pitchers,
Would tediously walk the gruelling nine miles,
To collect water from the half filled polluted river,
It was here that young Arlec, saw her dead husband Moses,
Their eyes and bodies frozen by fear, all they could do was shiver.
With burst blistered feet, which were now excruciatingly sore, raw,
They limped back to the safety of the aid camp once more,
Draped over tall spindly sticks, the multi-coloured wool blankets,
Of this widow's humble home, have sadly faded in time,
Under the hash fierceness, of the scorching sun,
Yet it brings great comfort, and sheltered protection inside,
As she frantically tries to console her new born son,
Quickly backwards and forwards, the discontented baby is rocked,
Its small mouth is cupped upon his mother's brown naked breast,
But alas a meagre diet of a bowl of rice produces little milk,
Feeling weak all she wants to do is lay down and rest.
Awakened abruptly by the frightening silent calm,
She gazes down at the infant, cradled within her left arm,
His head hangs to one side, the small body lies still.
Passing the opening, Jacob the aid worker suddenly stops,
His ears catch the sound of the loud piercing shrill,
Ripping the bottom of the wrap around skirt, trying to be brave,
In the make-do shroud, together they took Joseph to his grave,
No compassionate words he knew would ease her double sad loss,
Mounding the earth he remorsefully placed the small wooden cross.

Carole Beodricks Worth Reynolds

FOOTPRINTS

The screaming of the great birds before daylight
Told him it had been done;
The body carried to the platform
By the new moon's darkness,
And the chamber prepared,
As was the custom.

Today the moor stretches as
Far as the tamed, manicured fields allow.
The same clouds race shadows over it,
The same rain drenches the earth,
While buzzards cry and glide the thermals.
The burial mound beckons,
Dominates the screening heather as
Much as fence and information boards allow.
Imagination draws me to a people
Who left their mark upon the land,
Their dead to watch over and protect it.
I plunge my hand into the cist of time
To feel the wildness.

Margaret Black

Southern Alberta In The Fall

The blessing-rays of the sun spread across the fields,
Melting the tenderfoot snowflakes of the morn.
Canola, wheat, corn, and sugar beet, all the season's yields,
All is safely gathered in ere the scratch of winter's thorn.

Benedictive blue skies stretch for many a mile
Encompassing grit-gravel roads and prairies wild.
Cropped fields bordered by wire fence and stile,
Scarecrow waving like an abandoned child.

Chinooks warm the flatlands with their gusty breath,
Blowing the fallow fingers of skeletal trees.
The sap runs cold in a quiet kind of death,
Waiting for the spring, and resting in peace.

David Tallach

CHELTENHAM

Train ticket in hand, I'm not going far
Only to see a friend in Cheltenham
Cheltenham was just another place till my mid-teens
Just another place, not even in my dreams
Cheltenham became a paradise
It was a town of blooming flowers
The kindness of the people
You can marvel at for hours
When I left it years ago I felt an everlasting pain
So I go back to see it all again
Each departure back to Swindon I feel a broken heart
Oh to go to Cheltenham, to live there for a start
Whether seeing a friend or drinking the water
My feelings for this town I know will never alter.

P Edwards

Land Without Childhood

Forgotten land
Where childhood never was
What have you done with my life?

I am young, I am old
A middle aged babe
Life but a span
Between cradle and grave

Happiness and joy they say, exists
In a far off place
Strange sounding words

They keep saying love
These newcomers here
What is this love
And what is fear?

In other days
Will I grow, will I see many things?
Forget other things
Behind and before

Forget other times
I'll think instead
It's nice for a change
To be warm and well fed.

J Facchini

THE OCEAN ROAD

Come, let us travel on the ocean road,
Down to the azure sea,
Winding thro' golden corn and sweet-mown sward,
Where zephyrs blow with glee.

Come, let us travel on this sunlit dawn,
Adventure calls to me!
My spirit lifts as the seagull is borne
On wind above the sea.

See the small boats riding high on the waves
As the wild horses play,
Each bobbing along courageous and brave,
Tossed gaily in the spray.

Taste the salty brine, wind-borne, 'pon your lips,
Smell the fragrant flowers
Rooted in undulating sandy dips,
Drunk with heady hours.

Come, let us travel once more thro' this land,
Down to the sun-kissed shore.
Let us make our footprints in the wet sand,
Ere the tide washes o'er.

Let time stand still in this beautiful land,
Where my soul can find peace,
Where none can order nor make a command,
And life is filled with ease.

Gwendoline Douglas

THE MONSOONS

This year the monsoons never came.
We searched for clouds, but all in vain.
From blue toned void of palest hue,
The sun just shone; the wind just blew.
As choking dust clouds danced around
Upon the cracked and rock-hard ground
Our tiny seedlings battled through
For nature's clock showed rain as due.
But not one drop of moisture came
To herald God's life giving rain,
And so we watched green shoots decay,
Shrink up their leaves and fade away,
Whilst still the sun shone overhead
And left our withered crops quite dead.
For such a fate we had not planned
As famine grim spread o'er our land,
Destroying hope, and crops and herds,
Making our prayers seem empty words.
No stores remained from better years
To feed our young and stem their tears.
Our thirsty cattle fell, to die
As river-beds and wells went dry,
Till left with naught to drink or eat
We faced our fate in endless heat.
So you in temperate lands afar
Mark well what lucky folk you are,
Who do not have to search the sky
For clouds that mean you live. Or die!
Thank God for every shower of rain.
This year the monsoons never came.

Richard J Bradshaw

FISH EYE

Fish looked around
Acknowledged the others
Rocks, weeds, mud
But thought that was all
There was to it

Then along came a worm
That stuck in the throat
And pain suffered
Because of it

Without understanding
This wasn't enough
When returned
To notice life's water
For want of it.

Nick Colton

BEYOND THE HORIZON

Many years ago
I walked to school in a quite heavy fog.
Three yards to the right or left. I went agog
Toward 'ten feet' to go.

As far as you can see -
That is horizon, standing where you are.
Where you are standing orders near or far;
Near from a valley.

Standing on a plain
The distant rim is sinking in earth's curve.
Stand on a mountain, wide views you deserve.
View point once again.

Stand where you may be
In the open air, given a clear sky
Look up above you, how far sees your eye?
To infinity?

Your sight reaches where?
Your eyes reach the stars? Starlight reaches you!
Reach beyond yourself, find things reaching you!
Wonders everywhere.

Never be afraid.
Knock and ask and seek, there is something there,
Even heavy fog makes adventure where
'Normal' is betrayed.

Life has horizon.
People in trouble can't see what to do.
Lost their horizon, could happen to you.
What are your eyes on?

Elsie Norman

WHISKY 2

Darling little Whisky,
brave heart,
in this world so risky
you have played your part.

Happy little fellow,
friend to us and more,
we shall miss you sore,
when you go to the great hunting ground
where joys abound
and grand-daddy is found.

For the moment you are sad,
why you feel so bad
you do not understand;
but when you join the band
and your tail is no longer sore,
once again you will frisk in the sand
on the celestial shore.

Elaine McCulloch Smith

REGENCY LADY

Black, crested, smart barouche
Pulled by horses of cream,
Carrying a Regency lady
Through the London scene.

Cerulean, silken dress,
With long and buttoned sleeves,
Waterloo, cherried hat
The carriage rustles through the leaves.

Fur trimmed, blue pelisse,
Accompanied by a muff.
Velvet, half-walking boots,
She sits on seats of buff.

Brunette curls are clustered,
A few still peeping through.
Smiling to acquaintances,
Everything she owns is new.

A lady to be admired,
Of birth, wealth, and looks.
Her mother is so very proud -
She's caught an Earl on her hook.

A wedding of the season,
Everything fine and smart.
For that is their life's aim,
And the Regency's fine art.

Caron Hunt

DECREE NISI

Love floated out of sight
Day disappeared all is night
Nothing left nothing right
Spirit drained from the fight.

Never saw the danger sign
Another mountain now to climb
Living life all in mime
Stagnant as a souring wine.

Weather simply falling down
Lost my face as a clown
Cannot smile just a frown
Life's just a dirty brown.

As a dove with broken wing
Once a husband with a ring
Now a fool not a king
So no flowers do I bring.

You played it as a game
Walking me down lover's lane
Leaving me just a name
And a broken photo frame.

So this is life, this is fate
Waiting for divorce court date
No crumbs on my plate
Just a residue of hate.

David Watson

STREET CHILD

In the stillness of the morning,
See the sadness in her eyes.
As the world looks on in silence
On the child that cannot cry.
She's the victim of the tourist;
Sells her body, just to eat.
All her clothes are torn and dirty,
She has blisters on her feet.

If we bow our heads in sorrow
But then turn and walk away.
We deny her precious childhood,
Steal her innocence, her play.
See the child that is within her,
See the crime that should appal.
She's the child the world's forgotten,
She's the daughter of us all.

Help her face a new tomorrow,
Give her hope and happiness.
Help to save her from defilement,
All her suffering and distress.
If we speak aloud, condemning
All the evil that we see.
Give our wealth and our compassion,
Give her love and set her free.

Linda J Bodicoat

THE ABORIGINEE

I'm the Aboriginee
Killed upon this land
So that you descendants
Could take the upper hand.

Proud I was - to be a nomad
When Australia was mine;
Are you proud to own the homestead
Where nomadic bones now lie?

And do you hear our spirits wailing
Like the howling dingoes do
And a rustle by the wattle
When a nomad watches you?

Mary Rutley

THE LAMB OF KNOCK

In Knock I saw four rainbows,
Two were in the sky.
One was on a Cross and Lamb,
That I was kneeling by.

In Knock I saw four figures,
In pure white marble there.
Joseph - Mary - and Saint John,
And a little Lamb so rare.

I gazed upon the beauty,
And the tranquillity,
I longed to hold that little Lamb,
Who gave His life for me.

I saw a revelation,
More poignant than before.
I felt my heart uplifted,
By the beauty that I saw.

This was a shrine of Mary,
In this country town of Knock.
The centre point was Jesus,
The Lamb and Shepherd of His flock.

I felt so very privileged,
Surrounded by Lambs of Love,
As I came back from Knock to Preston,
To my PP Lamb of Home.

Jean Turner

THE OLD WHITE LION HOTEL (HAWORTH)

Couchant lies the lion in grandeur
Hard atop the cobbled street,
Memories harsh and mixed with languor -
Horses' hooves and pattened feet.
Sheeted cold in bleak November
With the crisp, warm smell of loaves;
And a midnight falling ember
From the stone-built cottage stoves.
Cholera and typhoid sending
Death amongst the infant poor,
And the Brontë sisters wending
Cross the cloud-black, rain-blown moor.
So the shadows cast their own shape
And the clock chimes from the spire;
So the seasons brush the landscape
With God's elemental fire.

Christopher Rothery

BEYOND THE HORIZON

Dark clouds are gathering, there is coming a storm;
Turbulence and wind as dark clouds form.
Thunder and lightning are there in the sky
But be not afraid, it will soon pass you by.

The dark clouds forming are there in your life,
The wind and the rain are the storms and the strife,
But as the storm subsides and the rainbow you see
You will hear God's voice saying 'I *am*, forever with thee'.

The rainbow is God's promise, His promise of peace
And from the turbulence and pain you will find His release.
You will find your protection under the shadow of His wings
As a glorious peace to your life He brings.

Forget not who I am, forget not what I do
For I am your God who has always loved you.
I will cause the sun in your life to so shine
For you are my beloved and my beloved is mine.

Don Mayle

A Spider Spins His Web

In a place
Where no man will go alive
A spider spins his web
No sun will glisten on it
No hope or happiness
Will ever seep through

The place
Where the spider spins alone
Is in a tomb
Beneath the ground
The tombstone stands above. Blank
With no loving message written
In remembrance of me

I lie in my grave
Pretending I am dead
Left only as a shell.
I hear the rain momentarily drip
As I watch the spider spin his web
In our place of solitude

The concept of time is limitless here
I could be two hundred years older
Or perhaps only an hour older
The spider stops spinning
And scampers away from sight

Did I dream of the spider spinning his web
Or am I deluded by the darkness here?
I am blinded by darkness so
Perhaps in the process of dying
I dreamt
But now I am dead.

H A M

BEYOND OUR HORIZON?

To thoughts that, given time, all things will change
The sepia shaded photos give the lie,
As buildings on the High Street's pavements range,
The same façade presenting to the sky;
Whilst people passing friends will still arrange
To meet again, before they say goodbye.
'As it was' is bound up it would seem
In unremitting cycle and a che sara supreme.

To hopes that, given time, we may not see
Massacres and murders headline news,
Give rise to fears that there will ever be
Recurring strife 'mongst those of different views,
Who paint the backcloth on the stage of tragedy,
Choosing chiefly shades of darkest hues.
Despite the pains that point to early grave,
Through saving others, ourselves may surely save.

To dreams that, given time, man builds Utopia,
No longer raising cities to the ground,
But fills them from the cusp of cornucopia
And turns them to where love and trust abound,
Where politicians cease to show myopia
Confronted with privations daily found.
These are but dreams and would such dreams suffice
To carry all to lasting, earthly paradise.

Mary Ryan

THE WHIRLING WHEELS

Friction causes fires
Wheels turning, burning
Pour on oil
As they whirl away
Tractioned to distraction
A spinning, whirling dream
Labour saving devices, abstract days.

The whirling wheels have eyes
That can see all around
They can see through all the lies
Only have slight contact with the ground.

Pour paint upon the wheels
And make a painting in the road
And look on in amazement
As the wheels become a rainbow.

I see wheels and still more wheels
The whirling wheels
Shining in the sun
Let's pour on some more oil
And lubricate the dream
Let's make the wheels the best
They've ever been.

Ian Barton

BEYOND THE HORIZON

As I sit so still, and stare into space
I wonder what life is like at another place.
The children of Africa starving to death
But people just look and take a deep breath.

As they stare at the sun, as they look at the moon
Hoping each day help will come soon.
A truck arrives, people move fast
The scamper of feet, and noise that should last.

As sacks are thrown onto the ground
People move in hoping food will be found.
People so weak they can hardly stand
Some crawling along on the hot summer sand.

The sun beats down they can hardly bear the heat,
If they don't find food, another death they shall meet.
As they crawl along, then stagger to their feet,
The more time they take, the less food they shall eat.

As they reach the sacks where food is lying
People dish it out, to men and women who are crying,
They remember how it used to be when food could be found
When children and adults and laughter was around.

So when we complain we have nothing to wear
Nothing to eat, nothing to share,
We should think ourselves lucky and one day we'll see
The future is ours, and help should be free.

Keely Pepper

SIZEWELL B

I looked ahead and was filled with dismay,
At what I saw in the sky today.
A dome so large, a blight in the sky
Towering above trees, so many feet high.

I know that it's progress, it's nuclear waste
But why don't they realise it's not everyone's taste
To have what we have had for so many years
Taken away, and replaced with a dome full of fears.

It's ever so safe, is what they all say
And so I suppose, they're the experts today.
It brings great rewards, with money and wealth
But did they count money as being good health.

I ask you my people, have you a conscience at all
Will you be here too, when the great dome doth fall.
It will topple and bend, and far out to sea
Will be heard the screams from people like me.

You might think me daft, or ignorant and blind,
But, I know what makes life pleasant and kind.
It isn't your nuclear power station ahead,
It's caring for others, and sleeping safely in bed.

Take a good look at our Mother Earth
What would you say she was in gold worth?
Should we take away things nature has given
Or, by greed and desire, and lust be driven.

With the ground all barren, and dreadful black ash
Our dreams and hopes finished, we must dash
To some haven somewhere, safety to find
By that time will you care, or even mind?

For over nature, great wealth must reign
With little thought to the outcome, or maybe the pain
For the plant they call Sizewell, our greed has driven
But will it take away all Mother Nature has given?

Tina Brewer

THE BITTERN'S WAY

South of ruined Bromholm
where Chaucer and Langland claim
a fragment of the Cross drew pilgrims,
lie Norfolk's conflux of waterways
behind sandy marram dunes
calling marsh birds to habitat.

West, a silhouette flaps idly by
in harmony with creaking mill-sails
landing in a hidden bed of raw sienna
on a rough reed nest on distant bank.
Heron or crane? No, it's kink-necked,
hunched, plumper and smaller.

North on a crinkling Broad
dawn-rippled, before boats come,
geese stir, water shrews splash.
A flotilla of mallard and teal
launch to feed in new light.
The bittern's voice 'woomps' to the sun.

East, beside mingling streams
emerge their young, beaks upward,
awkward on estuary legs.
Buff, freckled shaggy waistcoats
blend like thatcher's straw in
dense, thick, sun-guled reeds.

The fenland bittern is welcome,
rare as wild butterfly orchid.
Stay, marsh bird, safe in the sedge!
Be like the ravens in London's Tower.
No horn-headed Norseman will come
to plunder while you remain!

Dennis Marshall

YELLOW BELLY CUSTARD

A decisive battle in history by name
America would not do the same thing again
With virgin soldiers he saw their plight
Awaiting for the Indian might
A man of courage everyone knew
But a man has to do what a man has to do
Sitting Bull waits with a thousand braves
A signal is given, now descending in waves
The Little Big Horn was the place not to be
A test of strength to sign a decree
A yellow belly custard would run from the fray
This man who did not remains to this day
A symbol of pride, justifiable fame
Yellow Hair to the Indians, General Custer by name.

Kenneth Butler

Northern Sung

The moon rises white,
over the frozen river,
the darkness of heaven descends.

The palace is in shadow
below the jewelled night sky,
the carp swim in the pool, dark and deep.

On a red leather divan sleeps
the favourite of the emperor,
the favourite of the wind and rain.

I read to her
the stories of the red cliff,
they remind me of my childhood

in Fujian.

An incense burner by the great door
pale grey, archaic in its shape,
belches its scented smoke.

There, above the great wall
the heads of Tartars
stare from their bloodstained poles.

One day soon, who can say?
The barbarians will cross the wall,
pouring south, destroying cities.

A vase in a recess, pale celadon,
so elegantly fluted,
is covered in inscriptions.

Guy Brown

TO BOLDLY GO

To book a holiday and boldly go,
With bulging suitcases and travellers cheques,
First class accommodation safely booked,
And routes well planned from one day to the next.

A great adventure, backed by guarantees,
Insurances, injections and a guide,
Fully prepared by those who went before,
Going not to explore, but for the ride.

But think of Abr'ham, Livingstone and Kirk,
Men who had no one to mark out their way;
With nothing in their packs but faith and fears
And no resort when cornered, but to pray.

And those who turned their faces to the west,
Loaded their prairie schooners and set out,
Across the vastness of the unknown plains,
Not stopped by mountains, deserts, torrents, doubt.

Now are you willing to become a pioneer,
Who does not shrink from meeting something new;
Who believes that in God's Kingdom there are still
New places to explore, new things to do.

Who believe that God will keep the hope alive
To lead them surely on the unknown way,
Content to know that he has gone before
To show them what to do and what to say.

The night is getting darker, and the sound
Of wild confusion fills the air with fear;
Give us the grace to keep on to the end,
When your bright city will at last appear.

Michael Darwood

SPACE AND BEYOND

Calling you all
Is anyone there?
Beyond the stars
Will you ever hear?
Seeking you all
Tunnelling in space
Our quest for answers
Is sought by our race
What's in the future
What's our past?
Our history seems vague
And our time won't last
Calling you all
Interstellar friends are we
Come join with us
Come join our spree

Returning your call
Answering your message
I am your God, but
you won't cross the bridge
For you can't or won't
And between yourselves
You fight and cheat
And believe you don't
Should I visit you
Will I be feared?
Will I be exploited?
Or will I be scared?
Returning your call
Pausing in space
Perhaps I will come, when
There's love in your race

Kofi Oduro-A

TWO WORLDS - HAWAII AND ENGLAND

I sit inside - Shakespeare's sonnets and poems of a new generation,
Music from the European greats,
The bring and share of food,
The warm up and presentation
One world.

I sit outside -
The storm filled clouds,
The trees, native to China but common here,
Immigrants - as are the birds,
As are the people including me (mostly Caucasian here today)
These islands, these people
So rich in diversity
One world.

This building - too evolving;
Once hospital, now college;
Posters of extra-curricular activities,
Fabric groaning from constant use and cutbacks,
Students from heavy workloads and assignments,
Counselling on hand
One world.

I write -
Initial squiggles become a way
Of describing self, or, through metaphor, another,
Or of releasing bitterness,
Finding space for moving on - emotionally, creatively,
Into new life.
Words - free flowing or verse -
Vehicles of self expression
One world.

Barbara Hickman

THE BELL OF THE DATURA

Hanging there -
A sculpture
No human hand
Could manage.

In colour -
Some way
Between gold
And amber.

I see you -
In tropical alleys,
Leading to
White beaches.

But now you
Hang for me,
Ornamental -
Resplendent.

Sandra Lewis

THE GREAT STAIRCASE

Victorian splendour, elegant sweep
Of carpeted stairs, soft to the tread,
We climbed. Grand Hotel with deep
Pile stretching in endless red.
Era of gracious living, no more found
Today. Yet in the mind's eye viewing
The dignity, grave, profound,
Of those who fashion wooing,
With dainty feet the great staircase tripped down.
Handsome men moustached and smartly dressed,
Gazed enraptured at each gown
That the ladies' style impressed
Upon their eyes, discreetly averted.
The fluttering fans, beringed white hands plied,
And attention diverted
From every whispered aside.
We saw with delight the wide balustrade,
Still envisioning the glories past;
Warming to the rich parade
Of memories. Oh! May they last!

Evelyn Balmain

MILLENNIUM MADNESS

M illenniumania within its grip
I nevitable problems causing derision.
L oss of computer dates, more than a blip
L essons to learn, making the right decision
E ach and every one has to be right
N ever before has such chaos dwelt.
I nescapable, the answer's in sight.
U nutterable the pain that can't be felt.
M illenniumania is here to stay
M aybe to some, the huge cost could have been better spent.
A gainst the backlog of homeless and poor.
N ational pride (deaf to all dissent)
I njected the rich who shut the door
A gainst those who spoke with compassion
      (and were vehement).

R Castleton

THEIR STORY . . . LIVES

The 19th century war
bought the gift of smallpox blankets
to the natives
(who only slit one another by the tomahawk)

      . . . but the soldiers got them first.
Most of the Indians said
'We'll fight' but there were those who tried
for peace and a few settlers left between
who came to be called naive . . .
trading a culture before its time . . . into peace
when gaining land and only more
fed economic visions of the material mind
blasting to eternity an embarrassment
to the cultured kind . . .
who saw at each subtle twist and turn

      that the soldiers got them first.

Jamuna Charles

AD 79

No slow lava flow
Rolled into Pompeii on that day.
Only the crash from Vesuvius,
Then the cloud of ash,
Smothering down from the dark sky,
Holding all the sin and the sinners
Suspended in time for nearly two thousand years,
The pictures and carvings
Buried from human eyes.
But God had seen,
And God had acted
As a warning to the men
Of the nineteen centuries to come.

Maurice Bowler

MILLENNIUM DOME - THOUGHTS OF AN OLD, HOMELESS PERSON

Home, roam, home, dome
Where? When? Why, why, why?
Will I live or will I die?
Dope, rope, hope, hope,
Cold, mould, old, so cold.
Must try, sky, so high, so high.
A new age, a new page
For me? For you? For them?
A symbol, the cycle, full circle
Millennium, 'annus magnus.'
How great am I, a withered one?
All done, all done. A lifetime,
Generation, no fun, no fun.
Dome, loftiness, sublimity.
A cover, a roof. Give me proof,
Give me sleep, give me rest
As I curl, here alone, threadbare, ragged, roofless.
Sky, high. Try no more, no more,
Curling, whirling, life or death unfurling.
I close my eyes, no surprise,
Only lies - one dies, one dies.
Perhaps to rise? I'll close my eyes.
To rise, perhaps - to rise - surprise?

Anne Leahy

Worship

The spirals soar
To a slender
Pinnacle.
Harmony attains its peak
And draws me irresistibly
Upwards.
Can such spare and
Subtly blended
Symbols
Evoke the
Unfathomable:
The mystery of
Worship?

I stand there
Motionless
Before the painting,
Concentrated, absorbed . . .
Totally and suddenly
I find myself transported
To a new dimension,
Surprisingly -
Not as an outsider,
Rather, all is focused in
Recognition -
The stillness replete with
Assent.

The seraphim veil their faces,
Ever in praise
Before the all-holy One.

Am I part of the rapture?

Sister Magdalen

THE ABYSS OF LONELINESS

To drift upon a cloud alone,
Until your tears descend as hailstones,
Your feet have turned into lead,
The hair like snow upon your head.
Then solitude claws at your very soul,
And bleeds until you turn cold,
Its icy crystals cut right to the bone,
Carving out a slab of stone.
Thunder crashes all around,
But you are like dew upon the ground.
Lightning lacerates the air,
Encountering no emotions there.
Rays of sun are dazzlingly bright,
Still you are indifferent to their light,
Although they warm the chilly air,
A frosty glint is in your stare.
Trapped in a tomb of loneliness,
You live in a dark and cold abyss.

Pauline Uprichard

BEYOND THE HORIZON

It has just turned to dusk
The sun setting behind the horizon
Deer shadowed antlers red and musk
Skies God's artistic work black orange and crimson
Slender trees' branches sprouting
What lies further beyond leaves us doubting

An eagle hovering wings on high
Diving and floating in a painted sky
Assorted birds suspended in the air
Seem to think they haven't a care
Where does chirpy bird brain wander
Above the clouded horizon ponder
Planes at terrific speed zoom
Believe that it's all doom and gloom

Where do insects and flies go
Beyond the horizon there is hidden info
Funny beings possibly in green or gold suits
Apple blossoms and citrus fruits
Where do we look beyond the horizon
Can't miss the face of the setting sun

Ann Copland

Mount Sarno

Despair is written on his face
But still he keeps on searching
Digging the mudslide in a daze
No thought of stopping, ever.

The weekend comes, the death toll mounts
Torrential rain buries the village
Homes and possessions no longer count
Then the sun bakes the ground, hard.

The town of Sarno is the worst hit
As rescuers dig in clouds of dust
Only they are healthy and fit
Unlike the victims, found

Even the cemetery has gone
Destroyed by a river of mud
The days and nights are very long
It is a way of life, there.

Rita Fisher

TUDOR COURT

Babies tight in swaddling clothes
Grown-up clothes for older boys
They always have to do their work
They cannot play with any toys.
They learn to hunt and write
And dance and fight
And talk in foreign talk,
And babies die inside the court
Before they have a chance to walk

The women go to marry men
That are rich and handsome,
The men come to be friends with
And please the king
That's where they get the money from.
And in this Tudor palace there is a lot of dirt,
But before they move to the next palace
It will be a cleaning-up alert.

Christopher Johnson (10)

SCENE IN SUDAN

Under unmerciful
Sizzling skies,
Sleeping in squalor,
Famine and flies,
Homeless and hungry,
Fragile, forlorn,
Children in crisis,
Tattered and torn.
Caught in catastrophe,
Begging for bread,
Strive to survive
In the fight to be fed.

Pauline Pullan

A Man Sat By The Well

In this dry and dusty land I made my way,
To Jacob's well, in the heat of the day,
I go alone, 'cos the others they sneer and snort,
They don't mix with women of my sort.

I don't think about the future, I've got a past,
I've had five husbands, those marriages didn't last,
And now another man I've got,
But he won't even tie the knot.

As I approached, a man sat by the well,
He was a Jew as far as I could tell,
Another enemy, I thought as my heart began to sink,
How surprised I was when He asked me for a drink.

He then spoke of living water, said I only had to ask,
'Oh yes,' I thought, 'no more need to perform this weary task,'
'Sir, give me this water, so I won't thirst again,'
He then told me of my life, had this man heard something of my fame?

He went on to speak of worship, but He was not a priest,
He surely was a prophet to say the very least,
When I spoke of the Messiah, He just looked at me,
Then He said so softly, 'I who speak to you am He.'

I left my water jar, and called them in the town,
This time they didn't look at me and frown,
They begged Him stay, believed the words He had to tell,
In this dry and dusty land, I met my Saviour at the well.

Pauline Wilkins

NOAH'S NEIGHBOUR

Although I am escaladed on all sides
by frequently emended facts
which take me
far beyond the present
to my grandchildren's space and time
I cannot see how
I can circumscribe the evils
they claim
are killing land, water, atmosphere
and destroying our planet's future -
ecological pollutions
cause by
huge uncaring multinationals
in their drive to manufacture more
and more
from less and less
just for profit!
For how can I look beyond
the constraints of my day
to the far ends of the earth
and time's distant reach?
The stage is too vast
the time-scale prolonged
far beyond what my knowledge,
wisdom and mother-wit
can absorb and comprehend.

Dan Pugh

NAUMI

Your death has brought for me,
Such sorrow, but such relief,
I'd only seen you suffer,
Throughout your life so brief,
Now you can sit with God,
Play with your brothers and sisters again,
War and strife you will never know,
No need to scrape and fight for grain,
Hunger and thirst are your companions no more,
In the end only love and devotion were yours to eat and drink,
How could you survive on this earth, forever your
brothers and sisters salvation, their link,
Your seven short years were spent walking the bush,
Seven going on twenty seven, wise for your years,
looking after your two brothers and sisters,
To feed and clothe and wipe away their tears,
Hiding in the bush by day, walking by night,
Criss-crossing this harsh and unforgiving land,
Your little ones who loved you dearly would ask,
'Naumi when will we be home?' 'Not long now, not long now,'
was your stock answer as you took little Mua's hand,
You were adept at avoiding the military and the armed
                    gangs that roam,
The next eight months in the bush took its toll,
Malnutrition and death stole all your brothers and
                    sisters, one after the other,
Suddenly you were alone, no need any more for your
                    mother and father role,
Lost and lonely there seemed little point in living.
Having seen your parents put to death by the military,
Your brothers and sisters starve to death,
Relations, friends and neighbours suffer the same fate,

You can't remember rain in your lifetime, only ever the
unending sun parching the earth, your destiny and death
                                      have fixed for you a date,
You who had seen and suffered so much in such a short
                                                        span of time,
Lay down your body under a tree and quietly left it as a shrine.

P J Littlefield

TIME EVOLVES

Earth's essence of being deeply
 trenched
Beneath the ash of catastrophic
 times
Beneath the rock of avalanche
Beneath the darkened abyss of
 chagrined ruins that are no more
Betwixt the sky and earth no more
 to be the dream of man
His eyes now set on higher planes

Time conquers all, reality the
 dream.

Doris Hoole

Magic Carpet

If I could plan the perfect ride
My magic carpet sit astride
My soul and I would soar up high
Where man has walked and eagles fly
To see the 'people' of this earth
And understand their thoughts of worth!

Or would I need the perfect sight
To see the needs of those in plight?
Where warm true feelings for mankind
Bring together - heart and mind
Could time well spent for those in need
Give hope to all of race and creed?

Or will I need the perfect ear
To understand and really hear?
Give all my time to those who cry
With pain and torment - not walk by
For those who have and those without
Their desperation - full of doubt!

If I could have the perfect heart
Such wisdom would I then impart
To know, to give, count not the cost
For young and old and those so lost,
Think more of them, think not of me
Such needs would toll tremendously

Then I would down my carpet lay
To kneel upon and I would pray
A greater strength than I possess
To ask dear God to hear and bless
The needs of all on this wide earth
To walk beside in second birth!

Margaret Gardner

HEARTACHE

Tears begin to fill my eyes,
When I see the children and hear their cries,
Dying of hunger and dying of thirst,
Forlorn little faces, but who comes first?
Their tiny bodies so frail and weak,
Hardly the strength for them to speak,
No happy laughter, no playing around.
Too ill and too weak to get up off the ground,
They don't understand what it's all about,
To live in a country that knows only drought.

Dorothy Woodward

FLOATING (HELICON)

Oh to be suspended in space
Touching nothing, feeling nothing
Enjoying the luxury of it all.
The wonder and awe of this grandeur
Is beyond man's comprehension
Or their understanding, yet talk about their beliefs
Their hopes and fears, longings and despairs!
Which change as the years go by
Who knows what lies ahead
Who knows what it might be?
But, personally I would love to float
Float in suspended animation, no fears
No more worries, no more cares
Only the peace, the glorious peace
That no one can describe, nor the calm
Which accompanies it
Leading to glory, an unrecognisable fact
That awesome part of life, which we can only dream!
Floating as a bird, not swimming like a whale.

Tilla B Smith

THE FORCE

The force that's around, in all,
Never changing, totally ranging.
Born from nothing as a tide,
Rolls and rushes to rise and fall:
On the utterly small or celestial scale,
A patterned force, sustaining, arranging.

From the primeval, through aeons to move,
Harmonising vastness and the minute,
Iron, water, silver, gold,
Held by a force that none can prove;
Each living, dying, thing or being,
Filled with a force, never dilute.

No distance or time can change
The force that invisible stays,
Fills the universe and the void,
Ere all began from nothing, so strange;
A strangeness, was it planned, ordained,
Awaiting some divine relays?

Life, earth, water, fire,
All that is or was, will be,
Permeated by a penetrating force,
From the light of a diamond, or a man's desire,
Present on a cosmic scale,
In every particle that's you and me.

Nothing lasts, all things evolve,
Yet the force so powerfully stays,
Outlasting time in endless space,
And an enigma that none can solve;
For why and what is a force so subtle,
That mocks eternity, yet fills our days?

Iolo Lewis

NEEDS MUST

Aching limbs, sore feet,
Walking for me is no treat.

Till at the water stream we ladies meet,
To chat a while and bathe our feet.

A rest, food and drink is all I need for now,
Then I'll set off, I'll have to manage to get home somehow.

Anne Trapp

COLUMBUS

Stout-hearted, brave and true was he,
A prince above the tide of lesser men,
His eye could way beyond their world, their ken,
And way beyond the far horizon see.

The earth not flat, but round! Could he
Such strange ideas with gravity maintain?
And yet he raised a crew, and from the Spanish main,
Set sail across the vast uncharted sea.

On, forever on, towards the setting sun,
Beyond the point of no return, and still
He gave his sailors spirit and the will,
To persevere until their task was done.

At last, hope almost gone, they sighted land,
Rich in vegetation, luxuriant and green;
And where no European man had ever been
They walked ashore, and stood on pure white sand.

Natives, brightly painted and armed with long spears,
Emerged from the trees causing great dismay;
But smiles, warm greetings, and gifts, led the way
For friendship to dispel the sailors' fears.

Columbus dreamed of paradise on earth,
Till racial friction fuelled by lust and greed,
Divorced the tender blossom from its hopeful seed,
The new world from the promise of its birth.

And so he drifted into deep despair,
Humanity unworthy of his dream,
The journey's end had lost its guiding flare,
His eagle eye its awe-inspiring gleam.
At length he fell away, like his ship across the sea,
Beyond the slowly setting sun towards his destiny.

A K S Shaw

FROM CRADLE TO GRAVE

Just half a century ago
Good health was just a crave
Health-care for life was set to flow
From cradle to the grave

Then followed services for all
Free medicine plus surgery
Emergencies attended to on call
Less fear of illness was the key

So born then was the NHS
And decades of goodwill
GPs and matrons, and the rest
But sadly, later, to go downhill

Then came the Trusts with expectation
More chiefs, less braves, as some might say
It all adds to administration
One wondered how all this would pay

Some hospitals demolished and even less rebuilt
Matrons abolished, resources now extinct
Facilities outdated and decorations wilt
It's hard to tell when this all brinked

The doctors, carers, admin, all
Must feel the system lacking
With skills advanced beyond the call
It's time for solid backing.

Edward Roberts

THE LAND OF THE SCORCHING SUN

It was some time ago - yet close it seems
When warriors from hell, the Japanese.
Brought disillusionment and hate to bear;
A soldier once, he weeps for he was there.
Once water colour picture spelled Japan
For he had been artistic Englishman;
Washing the liquid green and peach relief
How frail a flower, an oriental leaf.
But beatings brought the prisoner great pain;
Would Nippon gardens ever charm again?
The little man once dotting his design
So innocently boasting fishing line
Beneath an eastern sun's caressing rays,
A soldier vomits now upon those days;
Witness to the yellow nation's crime,
Nightmares point with gall to a former time.
Tears are for those men who could not stay the course,
Collapsing like crushed blooms at devil force.
This western fighter never calls to mind
Quaint bridges where cool waters twist and wind
Nor pretty geishas with their neat feet bound;
Bird song dies as a bully's orders sound.
A mirage, beauty, scintillating blue -
It seems that merely savagery is true.
Now old, the soldier tosses in bed,
The colour he may glimpse a lone blood red;
His mates who perished through brutality
For them, can there still flourish artistry?

Ruth Daviat

Childhood Reflections

I remember
Days, not long ago,
When I sat and picked the cowslips on the hill;
When I searched the crannies for their violets,
And the buttercups for their gold,
Anemones in the woodland,
And bluebells in their 'bode.

I'd sit and make a chain of daisies
Gathered here and there;
I'd make believe I was a queen
And oh, so very fair!

All this
In days not long gone by,
When the world held such enchantment
For a child as such was I.

Barbara Crook

Millennium

Arrived at last, the millennium looms.
We, living now, are promised much.
Believe it or not, they're lifting the booms.
That's what they say, it's ours as such.

Happiness desired, for us eludes.
Struggle through life, the only way known.
They have never been right, so one concludes,
you can only reap what you have sown.

Do they plan to eliminate hate,
jealousy, poverty, the homeless plight?
They always say 'It's never too late,
we've got it in hand, not losing sight.'

It will not change, it never can,
they've got it made, it's theirs to keep
Can't have us spoiling the master plan,
can you enjoy it while others weep?

Maurice Wilkinson

DRIFTING

Through the opaque stillness of the window
the different transparency of the night
I see my domain
in the starry, crystal light

The time which has drifted, far beyond my reach
lies years in the distance, deserted from my fingers
Flowing down the midnight stream
where all the lost time lingers

I walk a mile for someone, who seems so near
but lost in the past
The life has run dry
and the entrance that will not last

I have achieved my goals and run for the stars
finally growing old and so I must die
I won the gold, silver and bronze, and now
the sun is setting in the dusky golden sky.

Nicole Purkiss (15)

The Berlin Wall

There it stood 'twixt east and west,
Dividing 'ossies' from the rest.
Built to keep the people in,
Separating kith from kin.

Hundreds lived in expectation
Of fleeing to their other nation.
Most who dared to make the trip,
Failed, or perished on the strip.

So ingenious were escapers,
Reports abounded in the papers.
Under, over, through the wall,
Why bother having one at all?

The 'modern border' redesigned,
Overnight, escapes declined.
The opportunists saved the day,
Professionals, who made you pay.

Then one day, like Jericho,
Perestroika laid it low.
Bits of concrete stained with tears,
Were bought and sold as souvenirs.

Five years later, all's serene,
And hard to see where wall has been.
Now the country's unified,
Let's remember those who died.

Gordon Haines

HUNGER OF THE AFRICAN PLAIN

An everlasting heat,
That spreads across,
Every street,
Starts fires,
And turns our soil yellow.
So no grain will grow,
And there can be,
No water flow.
There is no school,
Where can we learn,
And there is no place,
To hide from the sun.
We're trapped in a land of dead,
Where those who live,
Are never fed.
For in my life I've lived,
In this dry, deserted place,
But now the roads are coming,
And I fear for my race.
They say the land is no longer ours,
But what is unusable land?
Nothing but a pile of sand.

Lindsey Maggs

BEYOND THE HORIZON

'Little girl, do not cry.'
Her small black head
Against her mother's chest,
Sucking a tiny thumb,
Her mother was dead,
And so was everyone else,
She cried, alone and desperate,
Starving for human need,
Food, shelter, love, sleep,
Many passed her by,
And not one picked her up,
Painfully thin now,
And still crying,
She dies.
Not that she lived,
Born on a rubbish heap,
The cause of a rape, soldiers,
Her mother dead,
Nowhere to go,
What choice did she have,
But to die on the rubbish heap
And her name?

Rebecca Lawrence (14)

What Is Presence?

What is presence?
Something that belongs in remembrance,
Could be caused by devotion
that comes from the heart and your emotions.
Is it the mind of power,
that turns your life back into a flower?
Your life is full of flowing desires,
that are just like a hot burning fire
our lives are full of mystery,
made from the past, the future's history.
We come into this world to live as one,
to fill our hopes, dreams as far as beyond.
I wish the world could be at peace,
so freedom can be re-released.

Melynie Smith

AFTER THE EARTHQUAKE

After the earthquake Anya sits
In the leaking tin shed. Without windows
Northern winds permeate the bones
Inflaming arthritic hands. There is no food
To feed them but on one wall a piano
Brought back from the old days
And her grandchildren play clumsily
Embracing a lost culture; trying to revive
A creative spirit. Her daughter is weary
From crying and trying. She eats less so
They can eat more. After nine years still
No hope of a future. Her children struggle
To write in English because this is the way
To become part of the new world. Anya
Is gracious, serene and wise and sits in the shadows
The aid has come and gone like the earthquake
It has furnished officialdom with opulence
Made paunches fatter and left orphans
Exposed to the ruthlessness of extreme
Poverty. In the aftermath of shock Armenia
Waits. Not just for running water, electricity
Sanitation and food but for the right
To live before they die.

Barbara King

Rwanda

I'm lying up against a tree underneath a burning sun
The sounds of dying all around mingled with the chattering gun
My last food seems so far away can't remember what I ate
While I'm hanging on by a slender thread for others it's too late

I can't remember when last it rained the land is parched and dry
With a broken heart and helplessness I watched my family die
The famine spread across the land no plant sent forth its shoots
People dug beneath the ground to rummage round for roots

Then soldiers came amongst us with hatred in their hearts
And fired their weapons callously then did the killing start
Nobody was made exempt their weapons they let fly
Women, children and old folk were left in the dirt to die

Bodies were strewn everywhere their lives ebbing away
The scene of carnage acted out like a macabre play
Unseeing eyes with infested flies seem to stare in space
As soldiers armourlited spat hatred in their face

It's going dark about me, what's that shining light?
I see my mother; she calls me her face is beaming bright
And as I walk towards her my heart is full of glee
My war-torn land Rwanda is just a memory.

Ray Moore

EMOTIONAL FREEDOM

What was, was
Wilt to forget
Shed events to grow
When to let go, one knows
Alone or with others
Face fear to recover.

Alan Jones

Peace

Peace comes with the softness of a breeze,
and stress, pain and turmoil all ease.
It holds, enfolds and in its embrace kind
heart's ease is found and solace of the mind.

It is a greater, mightier strength and power
one we shall only know in that last hour,
and in its infinite compassion, wise and kind.
stretch out our hands to ease the things that bind.

Margaret White

ET'S SON

The man's eyes scan the page,
Could the young girl be that age?
Children abducted from the earth,
To alien clones do give birth.
Lot's of children with no name,
All looking quite the same.
Keeps looking over his shoulder,
Lots of kids who don't get older.
Will the earth the clones run,
Ask the little men in area fifty one.

In their ship like a cube,
Babies made in a test-tube
Ships from out the sky,
Bringing children who cannot die.
On their base high above,
Children born to sell their love.
A world just full of kids,
Where old age was under skids.
Will they father ET's son,
Ask the little man in area fifty one.

Colin Allsop

Producing Manure

Nature produces
From acorn a tree,
A living temple for abundant life.
She thinks
And is hoping that all can see.

Man consumes
From the tree of life he grows,
A living temple for abundant strife.
Producing manure
Yet he thinks he knows.

Paul Corrigan

CHILDREN OF AFRICA

Far away under Africa's hot, burning sun,
Okoth treks barefoot the long journey to school,
While Olivia chooses which shoes to wear
Before jumping in the Mercedes,
The 'driver' dropping her right at the door.

Okoth plays in the dusty school compound,
Already tired from chores done before dawn.
Olivia chats with friends in bright corridors,
Hanging up smart school bags on shiny pegs.

The whistle goes, Okoth enters with a great crowd
Of roughly clad children into one windowless room;
After the bell, Olivia's small, uniformed group
Heads for the well-lit, well-maintained classroom.

Okoth shares textbooks and is lucky to have a pencil,
As he speedily copies the copious notes from
A black painted wall;
Olivia takes out her new pencil-case, opens
Her neatly arranged desk and prepares
For the interesting variety of lessons and experiences
She will have today.

    Children needing, wanting to learn,
    But from what a different 'start'!
    Both having the right to education for life
    But what kind of education do they receive?

    Dear God - Oh, that they may learn the greatest lesson of all,
    That they are children of one world-wide kingdom,
    And that in this they have equal opportunities!

Jane Otieno

GLORY

Heroes alone, all unknown
They fought the good fight
Killed miles from home
In the stench of trenches
Devoid of joy and light

Bombs falling overhead
Blood-stained limbs of the dead
Lay scattered over ground
Bodies of these our heroes
Piled up all in mounds

Young and old united
Angels through and through
In the midst of time
From our hearts and lips
Your glories shall be heard
... Never to forget you.

Jade Draven

EVEREST

The tempest swirls around the fragile tent
where we rest before the ultimate push
to the top. We melt snow and brew our tea,
huddling for warmth around the lightweight stove.
Stomachs churning, we cannot face the task
of heating food. We spoon strawberry jam.
Tomorrow we must attack the South-West Face
Of the highest mountain in the world.

Our support team comrades can only wait
anxiously at the base camp for our return
as we attempt to ascend Everest.
The storm tries to throw us off the mountain,
the snow strives to bury us for all time.
Too excited to sleep, we await dawn.

No cloud now, only glorious first light
as night gives way to cerulean sky,
framing the majestic snow-clad summit.
We move as in a dream, deliberately,
climbing fixed rope, finally without a rope.
One step, one breath at a time; we are there!

Dora Stables

SARIGERME, TURKEY

Naked I came
from Aphrodite's blue haze.
Woman in black silk
peers through dusty rimmed eyes.
Wine and boughs enchant my sight
of cobalt colours, dimmed through
the sun's enchanted haze.
For this is a magical moment
of mystical charm,
that lives in the memory
of friends near and far.

A T Williams

BEYOND CONSCIOUSNESS

This fear of oblivion,
as I look at myself
from the outside.
The mind that does not know,
the mind that lives in death
far from reality.
Eyes travel ahead
like spotlights,
lasers fence with darkness
the unknown horrors.

On the operating table
personality disintegrates,
status and identity nullified
into a half conscious state.
There is a light
seen through closed lids,
blood-red like a sun.
The sea in dreams
leaks through eyes
staining pillows.

Everything is forgotten,
the magic flying carpet is a quilt.
Silence dominates everywhere.
Death leaves the room
defeated, only this time.
Life flows back
from the refrigerator
into the roses in the vase
and the warmth of my wife's hand.

Raymond Fenech

BEYOND THE HORIZON

If one has experienced hardships or even sorrow
There may be a slight clue, how the poor goes through horror
When people are starving, and walking miles for a drink
We should thank our blessings to God, that we will not sink

It just makes us think, how the rich gets richer
Where the poor suffer diseases, and to go through all the hunger
It does not seem fair, what even that part of the world goes through
When thinking of the happenings in Africa, and things they cannot do

If the rich can afford to drink champagne with breakfast
How will it feel to go without, even for food and to even fast
Just think how the other side lives through the drought
For God will honour those, who give up some riches without doubt

If one has three mansions, why not sell and give up one?
Give to the poor and suffering, then the good work will be done
Give, and sell a car if you have three or four
Give to the needy, give to the poor

We should know that starvation, has been going on for years
So, why not open your eyes, for those who know many tears
Those that are dried up with thirst, till death is nigh
Think of the children with ribs showing, till they finally die

Why drive in expensive cars or even show off to a friend?
Why not give, and share to the starving, before they come to their end?
Think of those people that have to carry heavy pitchers!
Especially walking with bare feet, for miles for liquors

Helping the poor is the richest gift, and even to sell property
There will be the richest blessings from God, through His Purity
Although, we cannot give rain, because of the drought they suffer
Pray that the rich can give, more, and compassion for each other.

Jean P McGovern

THE LOST PLANET

We are but minute grains in a dessert of shifting sand
Jostling, fighting, loving, working for a place in a troubled land
We invent machines to work for us and take control
But they can't read noughts and crash into a black hole
A heaving mass of humanity searching for the light
But almost always end up staging a terrible fight
A planet top heavy and bulging at the seams
Man's quest for peace and tranquillity is the stuff of dreams
Animals and creatures don't take up much space
But their behaviour is an example for the human race
While man struggles and squabbles for riches, gain and power
They get on with their lot without complaint and bloom like a flower
So let us give thanks for what we possess
Before superior forces invade to sort out our mess.

J Russell

INFORMATION

We hope you have enjoyed reading this book - and that you will continue to enjoy it in the coming years.

If you like reading and writing poetry drop us a line, or give us a call, and we'll send you a free information pack.

Write to :-
**Triumph House Information
1-2 Wainman Road
Woodston
Peterborough
PE2 7BU
(01733) 230749**